Joy is our Banquet

Resources for Everyday Worship

Keri K. Wehlander

THE UNITED CHURCH PUBLISHING HOUSE

Joy is our Banquet
Resources for Everyday Worship

All biblical quotations are adapted from either *The New Oxford Annotated Bible with the Apocrypha*, New Revised Standard Version, Bruce M. Metzger and Roland E. Murphy, eds., (New York: Oxford University Press, 1991), or *The New Jerusalem Bible* (Garden City, N.Y.: Darton, Longman & Todd/Doubleday & Co., 1985).

Page 63: The quote from Hildegard of Bingen is taken from page 77 of *Meditations with Hildegard of Bingen*, by Gabrielle Uhlein (Santa Fe, New Mexico: Bear & Co., 1982).

Pages 100-02: The image of "Bakerwoman God" is taken from *Womanpriest: A Personal Odyssey*, by Alla Renee Bozarth (San Diego, California: Lura Media, 1988).

Canadian Cataloguing in Publication Data

Wehlander, Keri K., 1956-
    Joy is our banquet : resources for everyday worship

Includes index.
ISBN 1-55134-050-X

1. Worship programs. I. Title.

BV198.W44 1996   264   C96-930293-2

The United Church Publishing House
3250 Bloor St. West, 4th floor
Etobicoke, Ontario, Canada
M8X 2Y4

Printed in Canada

 960005

For Curtis
maite zaitut

May you
have much

Joy!

April 1996

To Jean & Greg~
with love and gratitude
for your treasured friendship.
May you be blessed with
that which makes every day
seem a joyous banquet!

Love,
Keri

Contents

Acknowledgements

"Open our stories to any chapter: a friend will have a page there."
The same can be said of *Joy is our Banquet*. Various pages reflect
encouragement from a rich array of people who bless my life with
their friendship. To each of you, I offer my thanks.

A few special acknowledgements also need to be given. First of all
to Curtis Aguirre, whose patience, wisdom and love truly make my
life a banquet. To Jean Blomquist, beloved friend and gifted artist,
for setting a table of friendship where I always feel welcome,
strengthened and inspired. To Elaine Perry, for offering so much
enthusiasm, expertise and grace from blank page to completed
book. To Gary Paterson, for sharing his poet's understanding when
it came time for the naming. To Margaret Marquardt, for her
steadfast kinship, whatever the circumstances. To the General
Council Committee on Sexism, headed by Juliet Huntley, for their
support and suggestions, and in particular, to Leslie Campbell, for
her ongoing encouragement, and for our many conversations
regarding *Joy is our Banquet*. A final word of thanks goes to Ruth
Bradley-St-Cyr, Catherine Wilson, designer Gordon Szendrey, and
all those at The United Church Publishing House who brought
these words into print.

Keri K. Wehlander
Burnaby, B.C.
April 1996

Introduction

Keri Wehlander's passionate interest in spirituality and creativity has shaped her life journey. Her delight in language and imagery is rooted in her childhood correspondence with her grandfather, who wrote prayers in the form of poetry and sent them to her. Keri would write her own poetry and stories in return. Later explorations in drama and dance led Keri to seek ways of integrating these expressions into the worship life of the various congregations in which she worked. In her work as a retreat and workshop leader, she has sought ways to create space for the emergence of the creative "Genesis" spirit in each participant.

We are delighted with the results of our invitation to Keri to write a series of inclusive liturgies for everyday worship. As a committee we read and experienced these liturgies as we worked with her through their development. Keri's dramatic liturgical sense, her wonderful use of language to evoke gentle, yet powerful and moving images, and her varied and extensive inclusion of Biblical passages have created a rich resource for community worship and personal meditation.

These twenty liturgies will be welcomed as a readily accessible and usable resource for the many settings of everyday church life — committee meetings, study groups, retreats. The following are suggestions for enabling participants to be most involved and comfortable within the setting:

- the leader should be familiar with the entire liturgy before beginning; some activities require props or other preparation;
- texts that appear in bold are to be read by all; texts that appear in italics are just for instruction and are not to be read;

- the Bible passages are best read by several different voices;
- seat the participants in a circle if possible;
- in several of the liturgies there are responsive activities. In these we suggest participants be invited into a brief time of quiet prior to the activity;
- be sensitive to those people who may wish to continue in silent reflection during the activity time;
- sharing in groups of three is often more comfortable than sharing in pairs;
- treat people with gentleness and respect as the images and emotions evoked can be powerful.

We are delighted to offer this new resource to the whole church community.

General Council Committee on Sexism
April 1996

Encouragements

1

Fierce Patience

Gathering

Voice 1: We are a people of convictions, seeking to make a difference.

All: **And some days we grow weary.**

Voice 2: We are a passionate people, working for the ways of justice.

All: **And some days we grow weary.**

Voice 3: We are a people of vision, seeing the shape of how our world could be.

All: **And some days we grow weary.**

Voice 4: We are a hopeful people, believing in possibilities and promise.

All: **And some days we grow weary.**

Voice 5: We are a people of faith, searching to journey with God.

All: **And some days we grow weary.**

Readings

ISAIAH 58:6, 9B-11

Is not this the fast that I choose: to loose the bonds of injustice, to undo the thongs of the yoke, to let the oppressed go free, and to break every yoke? ... If you remove the yoke from among you, the pointing of the finger, the speaking of evil, if you offer your food to the hungry and satisfy the needs of the afflicted, then your light shall rise in the darkness and your gloom be like the noonday. God will guide you continually, and satisfy your needs in parched places, and make your bones strong; and you shall be like a watered garden, like a spring of water, whose waters never fail.

All: **On the weary days, may we remember to rely on the Source of Life.**

MARK 6:30-32

The apostles gathered around Jesus, and told him all that they had done and taught. He said to them, "Come away to a deserted place all by yourselves and rest a while." For many were coming and going, and they had no leisure even to eat. And they went away in the boat to a deserted place by themselves.

All: **On the weary days, may we remember to rest.**

LUKE 18:1-5

Then Jesus told them a parable about their need to pray always and not lose heart. He said, "In a certain city there was a judge who neither feared God nor had respect for people. In that city there was a widow who kept coming to him and saying, 'Grant me justice against my opponent.' For a while he refused; but later he said to himself, 'Though I have no fear of God and no respect for anyone, yet because this widow keeps bothering me I will grant her justice, so that she may not wear me out by continually coming.'"

All: **On the weary days, may we remember to rekindle our fierce patience.**

Response

Song: "Trouble and Beauty" or "As Comes the Breath of Spring"

Litany of Persistence

One: Like waves shaping the beach:

All: **Persistence brings forth transformation.**

One: Like seeds germinating in the soil:

All: **Persistence brings forth transformation.**

One: Like a potter with a lump of clay:

All: **Persistence brings forth transformation.**

One: Like a child learning the alphabet:

All: **Persistence brings forth transformation.**

One: Like an ant, carrying a grain of sand:

All: **Persistence brings forth transformation.**

One: Like a bird with the first twig for a nest:

All: **Persistence brings forth transformation.**

One: Like the rhythms of the seasons:

All: **Persistence brings forth transformation.**

One: Like the turning of this earth, our home:

All: **Persistence brings forth transformation.**

Blessing

May our hands be strengthened for the work to come,

May our hearts become fiercely patient,

May our eyes see the promise of justice,

May our ears hear the invitation of rest and renewal,

May our feet dance in the light of God.

Amen.

Song: "We are Marching in the Light of God" or "Canto de Esperanza"

2

Crossing into Genesis

Gathering

One: Divine Breath:

Each genesis daunts us;

Each sunrise rekindles us.

We cross thresholds into young stories;

One step sings hope, the other shouts doubt.

All: **O God, midwife us into our beginnings.**

One: We long for familiarities;

We recognize possibilities;

Rowing between the tides

of transformation and resistance.

All: **O God, midwife us into our beginnings.**

One: Our roots stretch tender into this new soil;

Our fabrics are patterned with new coloured strands.

This unknown country will reveal itself

one heartbeat at a time.

All: **O God, midwife us into all our beginnings. Amen.**

Song: "In the Bulb there is a Flower"

Readings

GENESIS 1:1-2
In the beginning when God created the heavens and the earth, the earth was a formless void and darkness covered the face of the deep, while the spirit of God swept over the the face of the waters.

GENESIS 7:11-15, 17B
In the six hundredth year of Noah's life, in the second month, on the seventeenth day of the month, on that day all the fountains of the great deep burst forth, and the windows of the heavens were opened. The rain fell on the earth forty days and forty nights. On the very same day Noah and his wife and their sons and their wives entered the ark, they and every wild animal of every kind, and all domestic animals of every kind, and every creeping thing that creeps on the earth, and every bird of every kind — every bird, every winged creature. They went into the ark two and two of all flesh in which there was the breath of life... and the waters increased, and bore up the ark, and it rose high above the earth.

EXODUS 15:19-21
When the horses and Pharoah with his chariots and his chariot drivers went into the sea, the waters washed over them; but God saw to it that the Israelites passed through the sea on dry ground.

Then the prophet Miriam, Aaron's sister, took a tambourine in her hand; and all the women went out after her with tambourines and with dancing. And Miriam sang to them: "Sing to God who has gloriously triumphed: horse and rider are thrown into the sea."

LUKE 3:2B-3, 10-14, 21-23

The word of God came to John, son of Elizabeth and Zechariah, in the wilderness. He went into all the region around the Jordan, proclaiming a baptism of repentance for the forgiveness of sins... And the crowds asked him, "What shall we do?" In reply he said to them, "Whoever has two coats must share with anyone who has none; and whoever has food must do likewise." Even the tax collectors came to be baptized, and they asked him, "Teacher, what should we do?" He said to them, "Collect no more than the amount prescribed for you." Soldiers also asked him, "And we, what should we do?" He said to them, "Do not extort money from anyone by threats or false accusation, and be satisfied with your wages." ... Now when all the people were baptized, and when Jesus also had been baptized and was praying, the heaven was opened, and the Holy Spirit descended upon him in bodily form like a dove. And a voice came from heaven, "You are my Son, the Beloved; with you I am well pleased." And Jesus was about thirty years old when he began his work.

Response

A Blessing for Beginners

The group is asked to take a moment to reflect on the beginnings they are/will be undertaking. Then, the group is invited to take part in a blessing of beginnings. A large bowl and towel are given to the first person to be blessed who then states his or her name and, if desired, names a beginning that is being faced. The person then places their hands over the bowl, and the person seated to the right takes a pitcher of water and pours it on their hands as a sign of blessing. As the water is being poured, the person doing the pouring says: "(Name)_____, may this water be a sign of blessing on what you bring to birth." The person who has received the blessing may respond with "Amen" or "May it be so!" The recipient then wipes their hands and becomes the one who pours water for the person seated on their other side. The water blessing is shared around the circle until everyone has received it.

A Prayer for Beginners

Unfamiliar seas again:

there's been a shift in the wind.

We wrap ourselves in chaos and possibility

and attend to this unexpected course.

We prefer being experts,

and the skill that familiarity brings.

Yet, something continually

stirs and surprises us.

We are always Beginners.

So, let us go with curiousity and courage,

with vision and vigour.

Let us journey beyond

these opening doors.

Ready to learn

and learn again.

Ready to embark

and embark again.

Ready to trust

and trust again

in the one who has loved us

in every beginning.

Amen.

Song: "To Abraham and Sarah"

3

Mending God's Tapestry

Gathering

Litany of Mending

One: Let us call upon the one who knows every thread in the fabric of our lives.

All: **God of every seam and stitch,**
Gather and mend us.

One: Let us call upon the one who embroiders new designs, who weaves new textiles with patience and delight.

All: **God of every seam and stitch,**
Gather and mend us.

One: Let us call upon the one who patches worn places with compassion.

All: **God of every seam and stitch,**

Gather and mend us.

One: We are the tapestry of God,

each strand important to the pattern,

each frayed end worth the mending,

every thread a treasure.

All: **May we hope in these words,**

May harmony be our mending.

Song: "Blest Be the Tie that Binds"

Readings

ISAIAH 43:5-7
Do not fear, for I am with you; I will bring your offspring from the east, and from the west I will gather you; I will say to the north, "Give them up," and to the south, "Do not withhold; bring my sons from far away and my daughters from the end of the earth — everyone whom I created for glory, whom I formed and made."

GENESIS 45:4-5, 9-11, 14-15
Then Joseph said to his brothers, "Come closer to me." And they came closer. He said, "I am your brother, Joseph, whom you sold into Egypt. And now do not be distressed, or angry with yourselves, because you sold me here; for God sent me before you to preserve life.... Hurry and go up to my father and say to him, 'Thus says your son Joseph, God has made me lord of all Egypt; come

down to me, do not delay. You shall settle in the land of Goshen, and you shall be near me, you and your children and your children's children, as well as your flocks, your herds and all that you have. I will provide for you there — since there are five more years of famine to come — so that you and your household, all that you have, will not come to poverty.'" ... Then he fell upon his brother Benjamin's neck and wept, while Benjamin wept upon his neck. And he kissed all his brothers and wept upon them; and after that his brothers talked with him.

II Corinthians 5:17-18
So if anyone is in Christ, there is a new creation: everything old has passed away; see, everything has become new! All this is from God... who has given us the ministry of reconciliation.

Acts 10:25-29a
On Peter's arrival Cornelius met him, and falling at his feet, worshiped him. But Peter made him get up, saying, "Stand up; I am only a mortal." And as he talked with him, he went in and found that many had assembled; and he said to them, "You yourselves know that it is unlawful for a Jew to associate with or to visit a Gentile; but God has shown me that I should not call anyone profane or unclean. So when I was sent for, I came without objection."

Isaiah 11:6
The wolf shall live with the lamb, the leopard shall lie down with the kid, the calf and the lion and the fatling together, and a little child shall lead them.

Ephesians 1:9-10
God has made known to us the mystery of God's will, according to God's pleasure set forth in Christ, as a promise for the fullness of time, to gather up... everything in heaven and everything on earth.

ℛesponse

A Quilt of Reconciliation

The group is invited to take some time to reflect on their hopes for reconciliation and mending in their lives and in our world. Afterwards, each person is given a patch of cloth/or an index card which can be written upon with pen or markers. They are asked to write a prayer of reconciliation, or draw a symbol which represents this on the cloth or card. During the singing of the next song, these patches are brought forward and pinned on a large cloth, forming a visible prayer for reconciliation in our world. This tends to work best if the large cloth is one colour, and the patches or cards are a variety of colours.

Song: "Song of Community" or "For the Healing of the Nations"

Blessing

May God, who clothes creation in love

Mend each rift and strengthen each seam

That threads of hope

> **and strands of healing**

May be woven wherever we may journey.

> **Amen.**

4

Witnesses and Storytellers

Gathering

Voice 1:   We are witnesses and storytellers;

We are part of the unfolding tale of faith.

Voice 2:   Precious words and sacred memories

are carried by every one of us.

Voice 1:   If we "Go and tell what we have seen and heard"

each one can recite a chapter, a verse, a paragraph.

Voice 2:   When we risk spinning these yarns,

When we listen and speak,

When we carefully gather these fragments up...

All: **We discover that there is good news all over again!**

Song: "The Spirit of the Lord"

Readings

LUKE 2:36-38

There was a prophet, Anna, the daughter of Phanuel, of the tribe of Asher. She was of great age, having lived with her husband seven years after her marriage, then as a widow to the age of eighty-four. She never left the temple but worshipped there with fasting and prayer night and day. At that moment she came, and began to praise God and to speak about the child Jesus to all who were looking for the redemption of Jerusalem.

> **All:** **May we, like Anna, be witnesses and proclaimers.**

LUKE 15:3-6, 8-9

So Jesus told them this parable: "Which one of you, having a hundred sheep and losing one of them, does not leave the ninety-nine in the wilderness and go after the one that is lost until he finds it? When he has found it, he lays it on his shoulders and rejoices. And when he comes home, he calls together his friends and neighbours, saying to them, 'Rejoice with me, for I have found my sheep that was lost.' ... Or what woman having ten silver coins, if she loses one of them, does not light a lamp, sweep the house, and search carefully until she finds it? When she has found it, she calls together her friends and neighbours, saying, 'Rejoice with me, for I have found the coin that I had lost.'"

> **All:** **May we, like the shepherd and the coin-seeker, be**
>
> **witnesses and proclaimers.**

LUKE 7:18B-20, 22
John summoned two of his disciples and sent them to Jesus to ask,
"Are you the one who is to come, or are we to wait for another?"
When the disciples had come to Jesus, they said, "John the Baptist
has sent us to you to ask, 'Are you the one who is to come, or are
we to wait for another?'" ... And Jesus answered them, "Go and tell
John what you have seen and heard: the blind receive their sight,
the lame walk, the lepers are cleansed, the deaf hear, the dead are
raised, the poor have good news brought to them."

All: May we, like John's disciples, be witnesses and

proclaimers.

JOHN 4:25-26, 28-29, 39
The woman said to Jesus, "I know the Messiah is coming" (who is
called Christ). "When he comes, he will proclaim all things to us."
Jesus said to her, "I am he, the one who is speaking to you." ...
Then the woman left her water jar and went back to the city. She
said to the people, "Come and see one who told me everything I
have ever done! He cannot be the Messiah, can he?" ... And many
Samaritans from that city believed in Jesus because of the woman's
testimony....

All: May we, like the woman at the well, be witnesses

and proclaimers.

Response

Spinning Our Yarns

After a brief time of reflection, the group is divided into threes and each person is invited to share a personal story of:
1. an experience which has shaped their journey of faith
or 2. an example of how they have been a witness or a proclaimer.

After all have had an opportunity to share, the whole group gathers again, and a basket filled with multi-coloured pieces of yarn is passed around. Each person is invited to choose a piece for themselves as a visual reminder to "spin their yarns" — to tell their stories. Members of the group then work in pairs and help one another tie the pieces of yarn around each other's wrists. As each person ties the yarn around their neighbour's wrist, they say: Friend, speak your stories, tell your truths.

Prayer

O God,

Keeper of stories and Weaver of dreams:

set our voices free.

Grant us the courage we need to be tellers of truth

and speakers of the sacred.

Unstop our ears, that we might recognize the wisdom

of the witnesses in our midst.

Empower us with your love,

that we might spin new yarns

with confidence and grace.

Amen.

Song: "Thuma Mina"

Struggles

5

Casting Fire

Gathering

One:	Day by day, it seems the violence will never end.
All:	**And we cry out: "How long, O God?"**
One:	Day by day, those in poverty are pushed aside.
All:	**And we cry out: "How long, O God?"**
One:	Day by day, lives are squandered for the sake of war.
All:	**And we cry out: "How long, O God?"**
One:	Day by day, the earth is sacrificed to greed.
All:	**And we cry out: "How long, O God?"**
One:	Day by day, we are overcome by the triumph of injustice.
All:	**And we cry out, "How long, O God?"**
One:	Day by day, God is witness to every act, every thought, every word.
All:	**And God cries out: "How long, O my people?"**

Readings

Reader 1
LUKE 12:49
And Jesus said, "I have come to cast fire upon the earth, and how I wish it were already kindled!"
> *Lights candle which is placed in the middle of the circle.*
Our rage, like this flame, has great power.

Reader 2
JEREMIAH 6:10-11A; 13
To whom shall I speak and give warning, that they may hear? See, their ears are closed, they cannot listen. God's word is an object of scorn to them and they take no pleasure in it. But I am full of the wrath of God, and I am weary of holding it in.... For from the least to the greatest of them, everyone is greedy for unjust gain; and from prophet to priest, everyone deals falsely.

Reader 1
> *Lights another candle.*
This flame of rage within us has the power to be prophetic.

Reader 3
JOHN 2:13-16
The Passover of the Jews was near, and Jesus went up to Jerusalem. In the temple he found people selling cattle, sheep, and doves, and the money changers seated at their tables. Making a whip of cords, he drove all of them out of the temple, both the sheep and the cattle. He also poured out the coins of the money changers and overturned their tables. He told those who were selling the doves, "Take these things out of here! Stop making God's house a marketplace!"

Reader 1

Lights another candle.

This flame of rage within us has the power to transform the church.

Reader 4

MATTHEW 23:23-24, 27-33A

And Jesus said, "Woe to you, scribes and Pharisees, hypocrites! For you tithe mint, dill, and cummin, and have neglected the weightier matters of the law: justice and mercy and faith. It is these you ought to have practised without neglecting the others. You blind guides! You strain out a gnat but swallow a camel! ... Woe to you scribes and Pharisees, hypocrites! For you are like white-washed tombs, which on the outside look beautiful, but inside they are full of the bones of the dead and all kinds of filth. So you also on the outside look righteous to others, but inside you are full of hypocrisy and lawlessness. Woe to you, scribes and Pharisees, hypocrites! For you build the tombs of prophets and decorate the graves of the righteous, and you say, 'If we had lived in the days of our ancestors, we would not have taken part with them in shedding the blood of the prophets.' Thus you testify against yourselves that you are descendants of those who murdered the prophets. Fill up, then, the measure of your ancestors. You snakes, you brood of vipers!"

Reader 1

Lights another candle.

This flame of rage within us has the power to confront hypocrisy with truth.

Reader 5

MARK 3:1-5

And Jesus entered the synagogue, and a man was there who had a withered hand. They watched him to see whether he would cure him on the sabbath, so that they might accuse him. And Jesus said to the man who had the withered hand, "Come forward." Then he said to them, "Is it lawful to do good or to do harm on the sabbath, to save life or to kill?" But they were silent. He looked around at them with anger ... and he said to the man, "Stretch out your hand." He stretched it out, and his hand was restored.

Reader 1
Lights another candle.
This flame of rage within us has the power to bring healing.

Each person receives a candle and lights it from one of the candles which have already been lit.

> **All:** **This flame of rage within us will be released.**
>
> **This fire of anger within us will be tended.**
>
> **This spark of conviction within us will burn**
>
> **brightly.**

Candles are placed in the middle of the gathering.

Response

Song: "I am Enraged" or "Jesus Christ is Waiting"

Litany of Fire
> **One:** O Divine, Fiery Spirit,
>
> When we subdue the spark of righteous rage,

When we submit to apathy,

When we smolder in self-destructive prisons:

All: **Teach us to cast fire once more!**

One: When we forsake the torch of justice,

When we forfeit the power of anger in the work of

love,

When we forgo the tending of truth's flame:

All: **Teach us to cast fire once more!**

One: When we choose propriety over prophetic action,

When we cling to structures which are sterile,

When we close the doors to dreams and possibilities:

All: **Teach us to cast fire once more!**

Song: "Rise Up, O Saints of God"

Blessing

May the fierce breath of God

blow through our lives

and set us ablaze.

May the brilliance of her presence

kindle courage in us

for every wilderness.

May the fervor of her calling

    continually disturb us

    and draw us forth.

May her fiery faith in us

    be the spark that takes hold

    teaching us to do the same.

        Amen!

6

Unbinding Fear's Knot

Gathering

Voice 1:   The Spirit seeks us:

Calling each name with compassion.

"Fear not," she sings,

scattering seeds of promise

on every timid heart's soil.

Voice 2:   The Spirit leads us forth:

Teaching us new geographies,

and uncommon mercies.

Each step weaves grace and justice

into the fabric of our actions.

Voice 3:   The Spirit befriends us:

Strengthening tender hopes and weary dreams.

"Courage," she murmurs,

unbinding fear's knot

and breathing us into resurrection.

Knots of Fear

After a period of reflection, a long piece of fabric or ribbon is passed around the circle. Everyone is invited to name a fear which limits them and tie a loose knot in the fabric or ribbon. Please note that these knots will be untied later on.

Song: "O God, whose First Creative Word"

Readings

ISAIAH 35:1-4A

The wilderness and the dry land shall be glad, the desert shall rejoice and blossom; like the crocus it shall blossom abundantly, and rejoice with joy and singing.... They shall see the glory and majesty of our God. Strengthen the weak hands, and make firm the feeble knees. Say to those who are of a fearful heart, "Be strong, do not fear!"

All: I believe that I shall see God's goodness in the

land of the living. May I wait in strength. May my

heart take courage!" *(based on Psalm 27:13-14)*

MARK 5:24B-34

And a large crowd followed Jesus and pressed in on him. Now there was a woman who had been suffering from hemorrhages for twelve years. She had endured much under many physicians, and had spent all that she had; and she was no better, but rather grew worse. She had heard about Jesus, and came up behind him in the crowd and touched his cloak, for she said, "If I but touch his clothes, I will be made well." Immediately her hemorrhage stopped; and she felt in her body that she was healed of her disease. Immediately aware that power had gone forth from him, Jesus turned about in the crowd and said, "Who touched my clothes?" And his disciples said to him, "You see the crowd pressing in on you; how can you say, 'Who touched me?'" He looked all around to see who had done it. But the woman, knowing what had happened to her, came in fear and trembling, fell down before him, and told him the whole truth. He said to her, "Daughter, your faith has made you well; go in peace, and be healed of your disease."

All: **I believe that I shall see God's goodness in the land of the living. May I wait in strength. May my heart take courage!**

LUKE 5:4-8, 10B

When Jesus had finished speaking, he said to Simon, "Put out into the deep water and let down your nets for a catch." Simon answered, "Master, we have worked all night long but have caught nothing. Yet if you say so, I will let down the nets." When they had done this, they caught so many fish that their nets were beginning to break. So they signaled their partners in the other boat to come and help them. And they came and filled both boats, so that they began to sink. But when Simon Peter saw it, he fell down at Jesus' knees, saying, "Go away from me, for I am a sinful man!" ... Then Jesus said to Simon, "Do not be afraid; from now on you will be catching people."

> **All:** **I believe that I shall see God's goodness in the land of the living. May I wait in strength. May my heart take courage!**

MATTHEW 28:1-10A

After the sabbath, as the first day of the week was dawning, Mary Magdalene and the other Mary went to see the tomb. And suddenly there was a great earthquake; for an angel of God, descending from heaven, came and rolled back the stone and sat on it. His appearance was like lightning, and his clothing white as snow. For fear of him the guards shook and became like dead men. But the angel said to the women, "Do not be afraid; I know that you are looking for Jesus who was crucified. He is not here; for he has been raised, as he said. Come, see the place where he lay. Then go quickly and tell his disciples, 'He has been raised from the dead and indeed he is going ahead of you to Galilee; there you will see him.' This is my message for you." So they left the tomb quickly with fear and great joy, and ran to tell his disciples. Suddenly Jesus met them and said, "Greetings!" And they came to him, took hold of his feet, and worshipped him. Then Jesus said to them, "Do not be afraid..."

> **All:** **I believe that I shall see God's goodness in the land of the living. May I wait in strength. May my heart take courage!"**

ℛesponse

Unbinding Fear's Knot

After a time of reflection, the knotted ribbon or cloth is passed around to the participants, and each one is invited to name something or someone that gives them courage when they feel afraid, and to untie one knot from the ribbon or cloth.

Prayer

One:　O God, where hearts are fearful and limited:

All:　**Grant freedom and daring.**

One:　Where anxiety is infectious and widening:

All:　**Grant peace and reassurance.**

One:　Where impossibilities close every door and window:

All:　**Grant imagination and resistance.**

One:　Where distrust reshapes every understanding:

All:　**Grant healing and transformation.**

One:　Where spirits are daunted and dimmed:

All:　**Grant soaring wings and strengthened dreams.**

　　　Amen.

Song: "Spirit, Spirit of Gentleness"

7

Holy Resistance

Gathering

One: Breath of Life:

           You call forth the rivers of justice

           When hearts grow rigid as stone.

All: **Who will answer when you call?**

One: You call forth the bread of compassion

           When society turns into wilderness.

All: **Who will answer when you call?**

One: You call forth the seeds of courage

           When thorns of corruption grow rampant.

All: **Who will answer when you call?**

One: You call forth the table of hope

           When greed is the hand that divides us.

All: **Who will answer when you call?**

One: You call forth the salt of new vision

When hunger is fed with despair.

All: **Who will answer when you call?**

One: You call forth and wait in the silence:

All: **May we answer when you call. Amen.**

Song: "Arise, Your Light is Come"

Readings

EXODUS 1:15-20

The king of Egypt said to the Hebrew midwives, one of whom was named Shiprah and the other Puah, "When you act as midwives to the Hebrew women, and see them on the birthstool, if it is a boy, kill him; but if it is a girl, she shall live." But the midwives feared God; they did not do as the king of Egypt commanded them, but they let the boys live. So the king summoned the midwives and said to them, "Why have you done this, and allowed the boys to live?" The midwives said to Pharoah, "Because the Hebrew women are not like the Egyptian women; for they are vigorous and give birth before the midwife comes to them." So God dealt well with the midwives; and the people multiplied and became very strong.

DANIEL 3:13-18

Then Nebuchadnezzar in furious rage commanded that Shadrach, Meshach, and Abednego be brought in; so they brought those men before the king. Nebuchadnezzar said to them, "Is true... that you do not serve my gods and you do not worship the golden statue that I have set up? Now if you are ready when you hear the sound of the horn, pipe, lyre, trigon, harp, drum, and entire musical ensemble to fall down and worship the statue that I have made, well and good. But if you do not worship, you shall immediately be thrown into a furnace of blazing fire, and who is the god that will deliver you out of my hands? Shadrach, Meshach, and Abednego answered the king, "O Nebuchadnezzar, we have no need to present a defense to you in this matter. If our God whom we serve is able to deliver us from the furnace of blazing fire and out of your hand, O king, let God deliver us. But if not, be it known to you, O king, that we will not serve your gods and we will not worship the golden statue that you have set up."

LUKE 13:10-17

Now Jesus was teaching in one of the synagogues on the sabbath. And just then there appeared a woman with a spirit that had held her down for eighteen years. She was bent over and quite unable to stand up straight. When Jesus saw her, he called her over and said, "Woman, you are set free from your ailment." When he laid hands on her, immediately she stood up straight and began praising God. But the leader of the synagogue, indignant because Jesus had cured on the sabbath, kept saying to the crowd, "There are six days on which work ought to be done; come on those days and be cured, and not on the sabbath day." But Jesus said to him, "You hypocrites! Does not each of you on the sabbath untie his ox or his donkey from the manger, and lead it away to give it water? And ought not this woman, a daughter of Abraham whom Satan bound for eighteen long years, be set free from this bondage on the sabbath day?" When he said this, all his opponents were put to shame; and the entire crowd was rejoicing at all the wonderful things that he was doing.

MICAH 6:8

What does God require of you, but to act with justice, to love kindness, and to walk humbly with your God?

Response

Micah's Invitation

To walk, to act, to love:

this is God's asking.

Humility, Justice, Kindness:

this is God's song.

A holy resistance

to any oppression;

An endless passion

for all good will;

An ancient desire

to stand in God's presence:

These are faith's rhythms.

Come, join her song.

Song: "To Show by Touch and Word" or "I See a New Heaven"

8

No Longer Silent

Gathering

One: Holy One,

       Keeper of all stories:

All: So much remains unspoken,

       So much is stilled, muffled or silenced.

       We fear the knowing we each carry

         and the outcome of it being known.

One: Holy One,

       Lover of truth:

All: No act, no thought, no moment

       Can be hidden from you.

       You bear witness to all:

         and you ache for us

         that we might do the same.

Readings

Reader 1
MARK 10:46-48A
As Jesus and his disciples and a large crowd were leaving Jericho, Bartimaeus, a blind beggar, was sitting by the roadside. When he heard that it was Jesus of Nazareth, he began to shout out and say, "Jesus, Son of David, have mercy on me!" And many sternly ordered him to be quiet....

Reader 2
LUKE 19:37, 39
As Jesus was now approaching the path down the Mount of Olives, the whole multitude of the disciples began to praise God joyfully with a loud voice for all the deeds of power that they had seen.... And some of the Pharisees in the crowd said to him, "Teacher, order your disciples to stop."

Reader 3
SUSANNA 1:7-8; 15-22A
Every day, Susanna would go into her husband's garden to walk. Two elders used to see her going in and walking about, and they began to lust for her.... Once, while they were watching for an opportune day to find her alone, she went in as before with only two maids, and wished to bathe in the garden, for it was a hot day. No one was there except the two elders, who had hidden themselves and were watching her. She said to her maids, "Bring me olive oil and ointments, and shut the garden doors so that I can bathe." They did as she told them: they shut the doors of the garden and went out by the side doors to bring what they had been commanded; they did not see the elders, because they were hiding. When the maids had gone out, the two elders got up and ran to her. They said, "Look, the garden doors are shut, and no one can see us. We are burning with desire for you; so give your consent,

and lie with us. If you refuse, we will testify against you that a young man was with you, and this was why you sent your maids away." Susanna groaned and said, "I am completely trapped. For if I do this, it will mean death for me; if I do not, I cannot escape your hands."

> **All:** **If God would not have been my help,**
>
> **My soul would soon have lived in the land of**
>
> **silence.** (*Psalm 94:17*)

Reader 1
Mark 10:48-52
Many sternly ordered Bartimaeus to be quiet, but he cried out even more loudly, "Jesus, Son of David, have mercy on me!" Jesus stood still and said, "Call him here." And they called the blind man, saying to him, "Take heart; get up, he is calling you." So throwing off his cloak, he sprang up and came to Jesus. Then Jesus said to him, "What do you want me to do for you?" The blind man said to him, "My teacher, let me see again." Jesus said to him, "Go; your faith has made you well." Immediately he regained his sight and followed him on the way.

Reader 2
Luke 19:40
And when the Pharisees in the crowd told Jesus to order his disciples to be silent, he replied, "I tell you, if these were silent, the stones would cry out."

Reader 3
Susanna 1:23a-30, 34a, 36-44
And Susanna answered the elders and said, "I choose not to do it...." Then Susanna cried out with a loud voice, and the two elders

shouted against her. And one of them ran and opened the garden doors. When the people in the house heard the shouting in the garden, they rushed in at the side door to see what had happened to her. And when the elders told their story, the servants felt very much ashamed, for nothing like this had ever been said about Susanna. The next day, when the people gathered at the house of her husband Joakim, the two elders came, full of their wicked plot to have Susanna put to death.... The elders stood before the people and laid their hands on Susanna's head.... They said, "While we were walking in the garden alone, this woman came in with two maids, shut the garden doors, and dismissed the maids. Then a young man, who was hiding there, came to her and lay with her. We were in a corner of the garden, and when we saw this wicked-ness we ran to them. Although we saw them embracing, we could not hold the man, because he was stronger than we, and he opened the doors and got away. We did, however, seize this woman and asked who the young man was, but she would not tell us. These things we testify." Because they were elders of the people and judges, the assembly believed them and condemned her to death. Then Susanna cried out with a loud voice, and said, "O eternal God, you know what is secret and are aware of all things before they come to be; you know that these men have given false evidence against me.... I have done none of the wicked things that they have charged against me!" And God heard her cry.

> **All:** Nothing is covered up that will not be uncovered, and nothing secret that will not become known. Therefore whatever you have said in the dark will be heard in the light, and what you have whis-pered behind closed doors will be proclaimed from the housetops. *(Luke 12:2-3)*

Response

A Litany for Breaking Silence

One: We walk the edge of silence;

we dread the consequence of truth.

Fear takes root and grows invisibly in us.

All: **And yet, it is said that we shall know the truth**

and the truth shall set us free.

One: We long to believe, but other voices haunt us:

retaliation, loss, shame, contempt.

This precipice seems familiar, simple.

All: **And yet, it is said that we shall know the truth**

and the truth shall set us free.

One: We stop and listen again,

searching for our own words

and for strength to breathe them into sound.

All: **For it is said that we shall know the truth**

and the truth shall set us free.

One: We cry out a syllable, thick and trembling

and the precipice gives way.

We choke out one word, then another,

and the veil tears in two.

We pry the thick fingers of fear

away from our hearts,

and we suddenly stand before a new wilderness,

> wide and unknown:

> but we are no longer alone.

All: **For it is said that we shall speak the truth**

and the truth shall set us free.

Song: "Rise Up, O Saints of God" or "Ba ni ngyeti Ba Yawe"

Blessing

May we leave the land of silence.

May we bring our truth to voice.

May hope be ours in every step.

May healing flow in every word.

May others stand with us in grace.

May God grant us peace.

New Visions

9

Mustard Seeds and Sparrows

Gathering

O God,

we are tangled in our schedules,

surrounded by demands,

caught up in the spectacular, the superb, the superior.

One day, we discover:

we never have enough;

we never accomplish

enough;

we never are enough.

O God,

in the midst of this chaos,

may the still, small voice tug at us

until we stop — listen — consider.

And, turning around in our tracks,

see ourselves and this world

again, through your eyes.

Amen.

Song: "Spirit of Life" or "Come and Find the Quiet Centre"

Readings

Reader 1
Listen to the voice of one who revealed a simple vision.

Reader 2
LUKE 12:6-7
Are not five sparrows sold for two pennies? Yet not one of them is forgotten in God's sight. But even the hairs of your head are all counted. Therefore, do not be afraid....

Reader 3
MATTHEW 10:42
Whoever gives even a cup of cold water to one of these little ones in the name of a disciple — truly I tell you, none of these will lose their reward.

Reader 4
LUKE 12:25-27
Can any of you by worrying add a single hour to your span of life? If then you are not able to do so small a thing as that, why do you

worry about the rest? Consider the lilies, how they grow: they neither toil nor spin; yet I tell you, even Solomon in all his glory was not clothed like one of these.

Reader 5
LUKE 13:20
To what shall I compare the realm of God? It is like yeast that a woman took and mixed in with three measures of flour until all of it was leavened.

Reader 6
LUKE 17:5-6
The apostles said to Jesus, "Increase our faith!" And Jesus replied, "If you had faith the size of a mustard seed, you could say to this mulberry tree, 'Be uprooted and planted in the sea,' and it would obey you."

Response

Time for Quiet Reflection

Litany of Basics

One: Consider the dance of clouds, the smell of autumn leaves, the gurgle and slap of waves on the shore.

All: **May we be still and know God again.**

One: Consider the harmony of crickets, the strength of an outstretched wing, the velvet touch of a purring cat.

All: **May we be still and know God again.**

One: Consider the deep laughter of friends, the embrace of a loved one, the fragrance of a treasured memory.

All: **May we be still and know God again.**

One: Consider the comfort of a sweater, the aroma of baking bread, the rhythms and melody of a favourite song.

All: **May we be still and know God again.**

One: Consider the common, present moment, and name it "holy," as God does.

Sowing Seeds of Simplicity

As the song is sung, pass a bowl of mustard seeds and invite each person — as they are able — to take one as a reminder of God's "still, small voice," found in the ordinary.

Song: "'Tis the Gift to be Simple"

Blessing

May the God of mustard seeds and sparrows

gently bless us

and grant us peaceful spirits.

Amen.

10

The Net was not Torn

Gathering

Voice 1:   Ever-creating God,

Lover of diversity,

In the beginning... there was variety.

Blues and reds, yellows and greens;

Firs and aspens, oaks and birches;

Ravens and swallows, finches and herons;

Lakes and oceans, ponds and rivers;

Mountains and mesas and valleys and plains;

Cougars and zebras and squirrels and sheep;

Dandelions, daffodils, orchids and roses.

And, indeed, it was very good!

Voice 2:   Ever-creating God,

Lover of diversity,

From the beginning, we in your image

Have also come in many varieties

And, somehow, this displeases us.

So, we do some creating of our own:

"Categories," we shout, "Divisions"

"Class," "Status" and "Rank."

And, indeed, it comes to be.

Voice 1: Ever-creating God,

Lover of diversity,

Begin us again.

Teach us to honour that which we are.

Enable us to love in your image,

To embrace diversity and agree, indeed:

It is very good!

Song: "Help us Accept Each Other"

Readings

GALATIANS 3:28
There is no longer Jew or Greek, there is no longer slave or free, there is no longer male and female; for all of you are one in Christ Jesus.

MATTHEW 13:47
"...the realm of heaven is like a net that was thrown into the sea and caught fish of every kind."

JOHN 21:4-6A, 10-11
Just after daybreak, Jesus stood on the beach; but the disciples did not know that it was Jesus. Jesus said to them, "Children, you have no fish, have you?" They answered him, "No." He said to them, "Cast the net to the right side of the boat, and you will find some." ... Jesus said to them, "Bring some of the fish that you have just caught." So Simon Peter went aboard and hauled the net ashore, full of large fish, a hundred fifty-three of them; and although there were so many, the net was not torn.

Response

Litany of Acceptance

One: We are a broken people because of our fear of diversity. We discriminate, we victimize, we humiliate, or we ignore because of our fears and our selfishness. We create categories of "acceptable" and "unacceptable" people. We acknowledge this and seek to be transformed.

All: **We remember that: "Although there were so many, the net was not torn."**

One: We are a scattered people, just as divided as the Galatians ever were. We need to be reminded of the

extravagance of grace. We need to remember that all
people have equal worth in Christ. We need to recall
that all people are created in the image of God. We
need to find new ways of living out these
understandings.

All: **We remember that: "Although there were so
many, the net was not torn."**

One: May we believe that there is enough room at the
banquet table for everyone. May we behave in such a
way that what would be said of the church today
would be that which was said generations ago: "See
how they love one another!"

All: **Amen. May it be so!**

Song: "Walls that Divide"

Blessing

May we journey together in peace,

May we honour creation's diversity,

May we live as a people united and reconciled

In the light and love of God.

  Amen.

11

Many Names

Gathering

Voice 1:   We call you Creator,

Voice 2:   We call you Almighty,

Voice 3:   We call you Eternal, and we remember...

All: **One name, one story cannot contain you.**

Voice 1:   We call you our Father,

Voice 2:   We call you our Friend,

Voice 3:   We call you our Lover, and we remember...

All: **One name, one story cannot contain you.**

Voice 1:   We call you Compassionate,

Voice 2:   We call you Righteous,

Voice 3:   We call you Glorious, and we remember...

All: **One name, one story cannot contain you.**

Voice 1:   We call you Source of Wisdom,

Voice 2:   We call you Amazing Grace,

Voice 3:   We call you Spirit of Life, and we remember...

All:	**One name, one story cannot contain you.**
Voice 1:	Whatever our image,
Voice 2:	However we call,
Voice 3:	This we remember:
All:	**One name, one story cannot contain you.**

Song: "God of Many Names"

Readings

EXODUS 13:21-22
God went in front of them in a pillar of cloud by day, to lead them along the way, and in a pillar of fire by night, to give them light, so that they might travel by day and by night. Neither the pillar of cloud by day nor the pillar of fire by night left its place in front of the people.

REVELATION 1:8
"I am the Alpha and the Omega," says God, who is and who was and who is to come, the Almighty.

I KINGS 19:11-13A
Elijah was told, "Go out and stand on the mountain before God, for God is about to pass by." Now there was a great wind, so strong that it was splitting mountains and breaking rocks into pieces... but God was not in the wind; and after the wind an earthquake, but God was not in the earthquake; and after the earthquake a fire, but God was not in the fire; and after the fire a sound of sheer silence. When Elijah heard it, he wrapped his face in his mantle and went out and stood at the entrance of the cave.

DEUTERONOMY 32:18

You were unmindful of the Rock that bore you; you forgot the God who gave you birth.

HOSEA 13:4-8A

Yet I have been your God ever since the land of Egypt.... It was I who fed you in the wilderness, in the land of drought. When I fed them they were satisfied; they were satisfied, and their heart was proud; therefore they forgot about me. So I will become like a lion to them, like a leopard I will lurk beside the way. I will fall upon them like a bear robbed of her cubs....

JEREMIAH 2:12-13

Be appalled, O heavens, at this... says God, for my people have committed two evils: they have forsaken me, the fountain of living water, and dug out cisterns for themselves, cracked cisterns that can hold no water.

ISAIAH 42:14

For a long time I have held my peace, I have kept still and restrained myself; now I will cry out like a woman in labour, I will gasp and pant.

HOSEA 14:8

It is I who answer and look after you. I am like an evergreen cypress; your faithfulness comes from me.

EZEKIEL 34:15-16

I myself will be the shepherd of my sheep, and I will make them lie down, says God. I will seek the lost, and I will bring back the strayed, and I will bind up the injured, and I will strengthen the weak....

II Esdras 1:28-30a

Thus says God Almighty: "Have I not entreated you as a father entreats his sons or a mother her daughters or a nurse her children, so that you should be my people and I should be your God? ... I gathered you as a hen gathers her chicks under her wings.

Exodus 3:13-14

But Moses said to God, "If I come to the Israelites and say to them, 'The God of your ancestors has sent me to you,' and they ask me, 'What is God's name?' what shall I say to them?" God said to Moses, "I AM WHO I AM.... Thus you shall say to the Israelites, 'I AM has sent me to you.'"

Response

Litany

One: O God, you live beyond us:

All: **And yet, you live beside us.**

One: You are known to us:

All: **And yet, you are mystery to us.**

One: You are invisible:

All: **And yet, we have seen you.**

One: May we hold these both in balance;

All: **Seeking never to limit you;**

One: Being ever at home with you.

All: Revering you,

One: Without fearing you.

All: So that we might be your many-named people;

One: And you might be our many-named God.

All: Amen.

Song: "Bring Many Names"

Laments

12

Withering the Green

"Now in the people who were meant to be green, there is no more life of any kind." — Hildegard of Bingen

Gathering

Voice 1: Wellspring of Life:

All: **Hear our cry!**

Voice 2: Women toil in locked sweatshops;

Children are beaten and ridiculed;

Men sleep in cardboard boxes on the street.

All: **The green within us is withering away.**

Voice 3: Speaking the truth is met with torture and

imprisonment;

Working for change is met with resentment and

retaliation;

Resisting injustice is met with threats and

interrogations.

All: **The green within us is withering away.**

Voice 4: Any colour other than white is heavier to bear;

Any orientation other than "straight" is a liability;

Any age other than prime is suspect.

All: **The green within us is withering away.**

Voice 5: Forests surrender to the violence of greed;

Waters wear thin with pollution's weight;

Creatures are extinguished, and no elegy sung.

All: **The green within us is withering away.**

Voice 1: Wellspring of Life:

All: **Hear our cry!**

Readings

ISAIAH **24:4-5**
The earth dries up and withers, the world languishes and withers; the heavens languish together with the earth. The earth lies polluted under its inhabitants; for they have transgressed laws, violated the statutes, and broken the everlasting covenant.

EXODUS **5:1-2, 4, 6-11**
Moses and Aaron went to Pharoah and said, "Thus says the God of Israel, 'Let my people go, so that they may celebrate a festival to me in the wilderness.'" But Pharoah said, "I do not know this God and

I will not let Israel go.... Moses and Aaron, why are you taking the people away from their work? Get to your labours!" ... That same day Pharoah commanded the taskmasters of the people, as well as their supervisors, "You shall no longer give the people straw to make bricks, as before; let them go and gather straw for themselves. But you shall require of them the same quantity of bricks as they have made previously; do not diminish it, for they are lazy; that is why they cry, 'Let us go and offer sacrifice to our God.' Let heavier work be laid on them; then they will labour at it and pay no attention to deceptive words."

GENESIS 21:9-10, 14-16
Sarah saw the son of Hagar the Egyptian, whom she had borne to Abraham, playing with her only son Isaac. So she said to Abraham, "Cast out this slave woman with her son; for the son of this slave woman shall not inherit along with my son Isaac." ... And Abraham rose up early in the morning, and took bread and a skin of water, and gave it to Hagar, putting it on her shoulder, along with the child, and sent her away. And she departed, and wandered about in the wilderness... When the water in the skin was gone, she cast the child under one of the bushes. Then she went and sat down opposite him a good way off, about the distance of a bowshot; for she said, "Do not let me look on the death of the child." And as she sat opposite him, she lifted up her voice and wept.

MARK 15:16-20
Then the soldiers led Jesus into the courtyard of the palace and they called together the whole cohort. And they clothed him in a purple cloak; and after twisting some thorns into a crown, they put it on him. And they began saluting him, "Hail, King of the Jews!" They struck his head with a reed, spat upon him, and knelt down in homage to him. After mocking him, they stripped him of the purple cloak and put his own clothes on him. Then they led him out to crucify him.

Isaiah 61:1-3
God has anointed me... to bring good news to the oppressed, to bind up the brokenhearted, to proclaim liberty to the captives, and release to the prisoners... to comfort all who mourn... to give them a garland instead of ashes, the oil of gladness instead of mourning, the mantle of praise instead of a faint spirit, that they might be called oaks of righteousness, the planting of God....

Response

Litany for Strength

One: We name all those who count themselves as dust:

All: **May they rise up and be clothed in strength!**

One: We name all those who have learned silence, submission or subjugation:

All: **May they rise up and be clothed in strength!**

One: We name all those who have suffered from violence:

All: **May they rise up and be clothed in strength!**

One: We name all those who receive the equation "less than":

All: **May they rise up and be clothed in strength!**

One: We name all those who are punished for their hearts of truth:

All: **May they rise up and be clothed in strength!**

One: We name all those whose spirit has been subdued:

All: **May they rise up and be clothed in strength!**

One: We name every thin seedling, struggling to grow among thorns:

All: **May they rise up and be clothed in strength!**

Song: "I See a New Heaven"

Blessing

May righteousness take root in our living,

May courage be cultivated in our hearts,

May hope be the harvest of our journey,

May the Tree of Life strengthen us,

now and always.

    Amen.

13

Sackcloth and Bindings

Gathering

One: In the midst of noise and chaos,

All: **We hunger for silence.**

One: In the midst of violence and loss,

All: **We hunger for healing.**

One: In the midst of despair and destruction,

All: **We hunger for hope.**

One: In the midst of lies and corruption,

All: **We hunger for justice.**

One: In the midst of division and distrust,

All: **We hunger for community.**

One: In the midst of critiques and our own fears,

All: **We hunger for acceptance.**

One: In the midst of confusion and commitments,

All: **We hunger for simplicity.**

One: In the midst of our slavery and our emptiness,

All: **We hunger for God.**

Readings

Reader 1
God hears our deepest yearnings, our greatest sorrows, and receives them with outstretched hands.

Reader 2
JOB 16:15-16, 7:11
I have sewed sackcloth upon my skin, and have laid my strength in the dust. My face is red with weeping, and deep darkness is on my eyelids.... Therefore I will not restrain my mouth; I will speak in the anguish of my spirit; I will complain in the bitterness of my soul.

Reader 3
JEREMIAH 8:18, 21B, 22A, 9:1
My joy is gone, grief is upon me, my heart is sick.... I mourn, and dismay has taken hold of me. Is there no balm in Gilead? Is there no physician there? ... O that my head were a spring of water, and my eyes a fountain of tears, so that I might weep day and night for the slain of my people!

Reader 4
JOHN 11:33-35

When Jesus saw Mary weeping, and the Jews who came with her also weeping, he was greatly disturbed in spirit and greatly moved. He said, "Where have you laid Lazarus?" They said to him, "Come and see." And Jesus began to weep.

All
PSALM 130:1-2, 5-6

Out of the depths I cry to you, O God.

May you hear my voice!

Let your ears be attentive to the voice of my supplications.

I wait for you, O God

my soul waits,

and in your word I hope.

My soul waits for you, O God,

more than those who watch for the morning.

Response

A Lament

During the specific petitions, a cloth which is easily ripped is held by the persons reading the petitions. After they read their petition, they will tear a strip from the cloth and hold on to it until the song is finished.

Voice 1:   God of sorrows, God of healing:

Hear the voice of our grief,

Hear the depth of our loss.

The fabric of life has been torn:

Our spirits are frayed and raw.

We ask, "why?" and hear no answer.

And, thread by thread, our tears fall:

the unraveling of our hearts.

God of sorrows, God of healing:

Hear the voice of our grief:

Voice 2:   We cry out for those suffering from abuse.

(a strip is torn)

Voice 3:   We cry out for those suffering from poverty.

(a strip is torn)

Voice 4:   We cry out for those suffering from injustice.

(a strip is torn)

Voice 5:   We cry out for those suffering from violence.

(a strip is torn)

Voice 6:   We cry out for those suffering from addiction.

(a strip is torn)

Voice 7:   We cry out for those suffering from betrayal.

(a strip is torn)

Voice 8:   We cry out for those suffering from oppression.

(a strip is torn)

Voice 9:   We cry out for those suffering from disease.

(a strip is torn)

Voice 10:   We cry out for those suffering from war.

(a strip is torn)

(Other petitions may be added.)*

Voice 1:   God of sorrows, God of healing:

hear the voice of our grief.

All: **Mend the threads of our hearts.**

Sow seeds of healing in our lives

and in the lives of all those who suffer.

Amen.

Cloth of Lament

As the following song is sung, those who read petitions and tore strips from the cloth are invited to pin the strips on a larger cloth of a contrasting colour, creating a cloth of lament.

Song: "Out of the Depths, O God" or "Kyrie, Kyrie Eleison (Taizé)"

Blessing

May God's compassion

>clothe us.

May God's presence

>mend us.

May the colours of God's promise

>be woven into our hearts

>>and into this world.

>>>Amen.

(*Note: The petitions in "A Lament" can all be written by participants, if they do so ahead of time, or they can be adapted for specific purposes, such as a service of lament for the women slain in Montreal in 1989 — Sonia Pelletier, Hélène Colgan, Nathalie Croteau, Barbara Daigneault, Anne-Marie Edward, Michèle Richard, Maryse Laganière, Annie Turcotte, Anne-Marie Lemay, Geneviève Bergeron, Barbara Maria Klueznick, Maryse Leclair, Annie St-Arneault, Maud Haviernick.)

Celebrations

14

Joy is our Banquet

Gathering

One: O God, hear our prayer:

Breathe kites high into blue skies,

Sow bright mirth into circles of friends,

Embroider brilliance into stars of night,

All: **And teach us how to joy.**

One: Paint the air with lilac's fragrance,

Feast the earth with gentle rain,

Clothe each creature with a whimsy,

All: **And teach us how to joy.**

One: Dance the seasons with new colour,

Caress each face into a smile,

Splash creation with your laughter,

All: **And teach us how to joy.**

Song: "Joy Shall Come" or "Make a Joyful Noise all the Earth!"

Readings

GENESIS 18:10-12 AND 21:1, 2, 6

And one of them said to Abraham, "I will surely return to you in due season, and your wife Sarah shall have a son." And Sarah was listening at the tent entrance behind him. Now Abraham and Sarah were old, advanced in age; it had ceased to be with Sarah after the manner of women. So Sarah laughed to herself, saying, "After I have grown old, and my husband is old, shall I have pleasure?" ... And God kept this promise with Sarah. Sarah conceived and bore a son ... and she said, "God has brought laughter for me; everyone who hears will laugh with me."

PSALM 104:24-26

God, how manifold are your works! In wisdom you have made them all; the earth is full of your creatures. Yonder is the sea, great and wide, creeping things innumerable are there, living things both small and great. There go the ships, and Leviathan that you made to play for you.

LUKE 15:4-6, 8-9

"Which one of you, having a hundred sheep and losing one of them, does not leave the ninety-nine in the wilderness and go after the one that is lost until he finds it? When he has found it, he lays it on his shoulders and rejoices. And when he comes home, he calls together his friends and neighbours, saying to them, 'Rejoice with me, for I have found my sheep that was lost.' ... Or what woman having ten silver coins, if she loses one of them, does not light a lamp, sweep the house, and search carefully until she finds it? When she has found it, she calls together her friends and neighbours, saying, 'Rejoice with me, for I have found the coin that I had lost.'"

PROVERBS 17:22A
A cheerful heart is a good medicine.

Response

Reflection and Sharing

After a time to reflect, the group is divided into threes, and each person is invited to share a joyful story or experience with the others.

A Banquet Meditation

An invitation so unexpected,

a messenger so insistent,

we accepted, in spite of ourselves.

We arrive, and delight answers.

We are anointed with laughter

and clothed with wonder.

Joy is our banquet,

and mercy our song.

Every heart is fragranced

by a dazzling, holy love.

Spirits are bathed and bright,

Voices share glad tidings, good news.

We dance the steps of innocence and wisdom,

and love this life again.

These gifts, so unexpected,

a giver so insistent,

we accept, in spite of ourselves.

Song: "Give to us Laughter"

15

Tree of Life

Gathering

One: Patient, mysterious forests

         Dancing, playful skies

         Glimmering, ancient waters —

All: **You blessed and called, "Good."**

One: Sleek, ecstatic dolphins

         Elegant, watchful herons

         Persistent, creative spiders —

All: **You blessed and called, "Good."**

One: Luminous, fragile shells

         Intricate, nurturing soil

         Drifting, brilliant clouds —

All: **You blessed and called, "Good."**

One: This beloved expanse of life,

         This delicate flow of breath,

Must be cherished to endure

Must be honoured that all may thrive.

All: **May we cherish and bless;**

May we honour and uphold,

May God declare: "It is good!"

Song: "God of the Sparrow"

Readings

Job 38:1, 4, 6-10a, 16, 18
Then God answered Job out of the whirlwind: ... "Where were you when I laid the foundation of the earth? ... On what were its bases sunk, or who laid its cornerstone when the morning stars sang together and all the heavenly beings shouted for joy? Or who shut in the sea with doors when it burst out from the womb; when I made the clouds its garment, and thick darkness its swaddling band, and prescribed bounds for it? ... Have you entered into the springs of the sea, or walked in the recesses of the deep? ... Have you comprehended the expanse of the earth? Declare, if you know all this."

Luke 12:24a, 27
Consider the ravens: they neither sow nor reap, they have neither storehouse nor barn, and yet God feeds them.... Consider the lilies, how they grow: they neither toil nor spin; yet I tell you, even Solomon in all his glory was not clothed like one of these.

EZEKIEL 31:3-7
Consider... a cedar of Lebanon, with fair branches and forest shade, and of great height, its top among the clouds. The waters nourished it, the deep made it grow tall, making its rivers flow around the place where it was planted, sending forth its streams to all the trees of the field. So it towered high above all the trees of the field; its boughs grew large and its branches long, from abundant water in its shoots. All the birds of the air made their nests in its boughs; under its branches all the animals of the field gave birth to their young; and in its shade all great nations lived. It was beautiful in its greatness, in the length of its branches; for its roots went down to abundant water.

PROVERBS 30:24-28
Four things on earth are small, yet they are exceedingly wise: the ants are a people without strength, yet in the summer they make sure of their food; the badgers are a people without power, yet they make their homes in the rocks; the locusts have no ruler, yet all of them march in good order; the lizard can be caught in the hand, and yet it is found in the palaces of kings.

MATTHEW 10:29
Can you not buy two sparrows for a penny? And yet not one falls to the ground without God's knowing of it.

GENESIS 1:31A
And God saw everything that had been created, and indeed, it was very good.

ℛesponse

Tree of Life

One: Ancient strength, this tree of life:

water, breath and bone.

Each leaf linked to soil and star—

no part stands alone.

Flight of an owl to form a branch,

scent of a rose to shape the trunk,

laughter of people to pattern the bark,

grace of a leopard to fashion a stem,

song of a whale to weave a root —

no part stands alone.

All: **May we revere this tree of life,**

and see it as God's own.

Walking our days, mindful of all —

for no part stands alone.

Song: "Into the Unshaped Silence"

16

Friendship's Table

Gathering

Voice 1:   Open our stories to any chapter:

A friend will have a page there.

Voice 2:   Look closely at our vigorous roots:

Companions nourished what holds us.

Voice 3:   Ask about our migrations, our paths:

Strangers became neighbours became loved ones.

Voice 4:   Listen to the cadence of our song:

A symphony of lives soars through each note.

Voice 5:   Watch us shelter beneath soft wings:

Friendship gentles our weariness.

Voice 6:   Discover our tables set with bread and laughter:

For we share what we have received.

Voice 7:   Sift the sands of daily journeys:

The grains of God's kinship glimmer everywhere.

Song: "Blest be the Tie that Binds" or "Song of Community"

Readings

EXODUS 17:11-12
Whenever Moses held up his hand, Israel prevailed; and whenever he lowered his hand, Amalek prevailed. But Moses' hands grew weary; so they took a stone and put it under him, and he sat on it. Aaron and Hur held up his hands, one on one side, and the other on the other side; so his hands were steady until the sun set.

JOHN 12:1-3
Six days before the Passover Jesus came to Bethany, the home of Lazarus, whom he had raised from the dead. There they gave a dinner for him. Martha served, and Lazarus was one of those at the table with him. Mary took a pound of costly perfume made of pure nard, anointed Jesus' feet, and wiped them with her hair. The house was filled with the fragrance of the perfume.

ISAIAH 41:8-10
Israel, my servant, Jacob, whom I have chosen, the offspring of Abraham, my friend; you whom I took from the ends of the earth, and called from its farthest corners, saying to you, "You are my servant, I have chosen you and not cast you off"; do not fear, for I am with you, do not be afraid, for I am your God.

PROVERBS 18:24
...a true friend sticks closer than one's nearest kin.

RUTH 1:16-19
Ruth said to Naomi, "Do not press me to leave you or to turn back from following you! Where you go, I will go; where you lodge, I will lodge; your people shall be my people, and your God my God.

Where you die, I will die — there will I be buried. May God do thus and so to me, and more as well, if even death parts me from you!" When Naomi saw that she was determined to go with her, she said no more to her. So the two of them went on until they came to Bethlehem.

JOHN 15:15
And Jesus said, "I do not call you servants... but I have called you friends."

Response

Prayer

One: Gentle, Holy Friend:

we give you thanks that we are not alone.

You companion our every path:

you treasure our minutes and days.

You clothe us in your love.

All: **Gentle, Holy Friend:**

we give you thanks that we are not alone.

One: Beloved ones brighten our lives and our seasons;

trusted ones give anchor in tumult and bluster;

spirited ones strengthen our laughter and songs.

All: Gentle, Holy Friend:

we give you thanks that we are not alone.

One: Our hands have offered their comfort and welcome;

our hearts have listened with wisdom and grace;

our spirits have shared in the journeys and tellings.

All: Gentle, Holy Friend:

we give you thanks that we are not alone. Amen.

Song: "The Servant Song"

Blessings

17

Plain Blessings

Gathering

God, our Maker:

Your open hands of grace

Sow us with many generosities.

You offer these ordinary treasures

Simply, and without demand.

We who receive

Do so with recognition

and delight;

Or we wander dissatisfied

and forgetful.

O God,

Grant us the choice of gratitude.

Transform our hearts into generous soil.

Make us ready to welcome,

Ready with praise

for every plain blessing.

Amen.

Song: "Teach me, God, to Wonder"

Readings

DEUTERONOMY 8:12-14
When you have eaten your fill and have built fine houses and live in them, and when your herds and flocks have multiplied, and your silver and gold is multiplied, and all that you have is multiplied, then do not exalt yourself ... and forget your God.

PSALM 139:14
O God, I praise you, for I am fearfully and wonderfully made. Wonderful are your works; that I know very well.

LUKE 17:11-19
On the way to Jerusalem Jesus was going through the region between Samaria and Galilee. As he entered a village, ten lepers approached him. Keeping their distance, they called out, saying, "Jesus, Master, have mercy on us!" When he saw them, he said to them, "Go and show yourselves to the priests." And as they went, they were made clean. Then one of them, when he saw that he was healed, turned back, praising God with a loud voice. He prostrated himself at Jesus' feet and thanked him. And he was a Samaritan.

Then Jesus asked, "Were not ten made clean? But the other nine, where are they? Was none of them found to return and give praise except this foreigner?" Then he said to him, "Get up and go your way; your faith has made you well."

PSALM 9:1-2
I will give thanks to you, O God, with my whole heart; I will tell of all your wonderful deeds. I will be glad and rejoice in you; I will sing praise to your name, O Most High.

JEREMIAH 31:12, 14B
They shall come and sing aloud on the height of Zion, and they shall be radiant over the goodness of God, over the grain, the wine, and the oil, and over the young of the flock and the herd; and their life shall become like a watered garden... and my people shall be satisfied with my bounty, says God.

Response

Litany

One: To wake from sleep into this day —

All: **Is gift enough for thanks.**

One: To hear a child's delight in laughter —

All: **Is gift enough for thanks.**

One: To sip a glass of clean, cold water —

All: **Is gift enough for thanks.**

One: To watch the sunset paint the sky —

All: **Is gift enough for thanks.**

One: To share a moment with a friend —

All: **Is gift enough for thanks.**

One: To smell the fragrance of moist soil —

All: **Is gift enough for thanks.**

One: To feel the comfort of clean clothing —

All: **Is gift enough for thanks.**

One: To form the words that make a prayer —

All: **Is gift enough for thanks.**

Song: "For all your Goodness, God"

18

Coin Considerations

Gathering

One: Structures of budgets,

Cycles of bills,

Seasons of spending

Fascinate and frighten us.

All: How can we sing God's song in this land?

One: Climates of wealth,

Chasms of poverty,

Committees of reckoning

Concern and confront us.

All: How can we sing God's song in this land?

One: Recessions and reductions,

Banking and balancing,

Credits and calculations

Subjugate and startle us.

All: **How can we sing God's song in this land?**

One: Divide and conquer our fear,

            Multiply our wisdom,

            Subtract our apprehension,

            Add justice and compassion:

All: **So that we can sing God's song in this land.**

Song: "For the Fruit of all Creation"

Readings

EXODUS 22:25-27

And God said to Moses: "If anyone lends money to my people, to the poor among you, you shall not deal with them as a creditor; you shall not exact interest from them. If you take your neighbour's cloak in pawn, you shall restore it before the sun goes down; for it may be your neighbour's only clothing to use as cover; in what else shall that person sleep? And if your neighbour cries out to me, I will listen, for I am compassionate.

GENESIS 28:18-19A, 20-22

Jacob rose early in the morning, and he took the stone that he had put under his head and set it up for a pillar and poured oil on the top of it. He called that place Bethel.... Then Jacob made a vow, saying, "If God will be with me, and will keep me in this way that I go, and will give me bread to eat and clothing to wear, so that I come again to my family's house in peace, then I will worship God; and this stone, which I have set up for a pillar, shall be God's house; and of all that you give me I will surely give one tenth to you."

Luke 16:13

No slave can serve two masters; for a slave will either hate the one and love the other, or be devoted to the one and despise the other. You cannot serve God and wealth.

Isaiah 55:1

Ho, everyone who thirsts, come to the waters; and you that have no money, come, buy and eat! Come, buy... without money and without price.

Luke 19:1-9

Jesus entered Jericho and was passing through it. A man was there named Zacchaeus; he was a chief tax collector and was rich. He was trying to see who Jesus was, but on account of the crowd he could not, because he was short in stature. So he ran ahead and climbed a sycamore tree to see Jesus, because he was going to pass that way. When Jesus came to the place, he looked up and said to him, "Zacchaeus, hurry and come down; for I must stay at your house today." So he hurried down and was happy to welcome him. All who saw it began to grumble and said, "He has gone to be the guest of one who is a sinner." Zacchaeus stood there and said to Jesus, "Look, half of my possessions I will give to the poor; and if I have defrauded anyone of anything, I will pay back four times as much." Then Jesus said to him, "Today salvation has come to this house."

Deuteronomy 30:19

I call heaven and earth to witness... that I have set before you life and death, blessings and curses. Therefore, choose life so that you and your descendants may live.

ℛ*esponse*

A Penny For Your Thoughts

A basket is passed around, and each person is invited to place a penny in the basket and name how money can be a curse in life. Once everyone has had a chance to do this, the basket is passed around again, and this time, each person is invited to take a penny from the basket and name how money can be a blessing in life.

Prayer

One: God of all hope:

All: **Hear our prayer.**

One: When money becomes a prison:

All: **Free us to choose life.**

One: Where wealth turns into addiction:

All: **Free us to choose life.**

One: When income determines worth:

All: **Free us to choose life.**

One: Where poverty equals invisibility:

All: **Free us to choose life.**

One: When economies deepen injustice:

All: **Free us to choose life.**

One: Where greed invents new oppressions:

All: **Free us to choose life.**

One: When finance rules every decision:

All: Free us to choose life.

One: Where consumption replaces compassion:

All: Free us to choose life. Amen.

Song: "Bless and Keep us, God"

19

Bread of Blessing

Gathering

Confessing and Proclaiming Grace

Voice 1: Bakerwoman God,

We are your bread of blessing:

All: **We who have been patiently kneaded by your strong and kind hands,**

We who have been filled with the leaven of faith,

With the seasoning of love.

All this we know:

And yet, we choose to turn away from you.

Voice 1: Your seeds of promise and imagination,

Planted deep within us

Remain dormant because we are afraid.

Voice 2: Your harvest of abundance, offered freely,

We hoard and store up for ourselves,

Leaving only crumbs to be fought over.

All: **You call to us,**

And your voice is the sweet aroma of baking

bread.

Voice 1:   But we do not follow.

We choose instead the leaven of success,

The salt of apathy,

The fragrance of power.

Voice 2:   We become impatient because the raw, unbaked

promise of justice

Takes time to rise among us,

And our passion turns to cynicism.

Voice 1:   We choose the comfort of familiarity over the

challenge of diversity,

And insist that the scattered grains of your body

remain scattered.

Voice 2:   We translate our deep hunger for you

Into the need for:

a new experience,

a new purchase,

a new expert,

a new style.

All:	**Bakerwoman God,**
	We ask your forgiveness.
Voice 1:	Breathe your fire into our hearts.
Voice 2:	Transform us.
Voice 1:	Remake us.
Voice 2:	Fill our emptiness with your love.
All:	**Bakerwoman God,**
	We are patiently kneaded by your strong and kind hands.
	We are filled with the seasoning of faith.
	We are forgiven and made whole again.
	We are your bread of blessing.
	And your leaven of love is rising within us,
	Transforming us into all that is meant to be shared.
	For this we give you thanks! Amen.

Readings

EXODUS 16:11-15, 31

And God spoke to Moses, and said, "I have heard the complaining of the Israelites; say to them, 'At twilight you shall eat meat, and in the morning you shall have your fill of bread; then you shall know that I am your God.'" In the evening quails came up and covered the camp; and in the morning there was a layer of dew around the camp. When the layer of dew lifted, there on the surface of the wilderness was a fine flaky substance, as fine as frost on the ground. When the Israelites saw it, they said to one another, "What is it?" For they did not know what it was. Moses said to them, "It is the bread that God has given you to eat."...And the house of Israel called it manna; it was like coriander seed, white, and the taste of it was like wafers made with honey.

LUKE 13:20-21

And Jesus said, "To what shall I compare the realm of God? It is like yeast that a woman took and mixed in with three measures of flour until all of it was leavened."

JOHN 6:3-5, 7-13

Jesus went up the mountain and sat down there with his disciples. Now the Passover, the festival of the Jews, was near. When he looked up and saw a large crowd coming towards him, Jesus said to Philip, "Where are we to buy bread for these people to eat?" ... Philip answered him, "Six months' wages would not buy enough bread for each of them to get a little." One of his disciples, Andrew, Simon Peter's brother, said to him, "There is a boy here who has five barley loaves and two fish. But what are they among so many people?" Jesus said, "Make the people sit down." Now there was much grass in the place; so they sat down, about five thousand in all. Then Jesus took the loaves, and when he had given thanks, he distributed them to those who were seated; so also the fish, as much as they wanted. When they were satisfied, he told his disciples, "Gather up the fragments left over, so that nothing may be lost." So they gathered them up, and from the fragments of the five barley loaves, left by those who had eaten, they filled twelve baskets.

ℛ*esponse*

Song: "All Who Hunger"

Sharing of Bread and Stories

An opportunity for the group to share some form of bread together and talk informally: perhaps answering the question, "What has fed you since we last were together?"

Blessing

May we sow seeds of justice,

May we nurture holy visions,

May we harvest gentle wisdom,

May patience be our grain.

May we mix in grace and courage,

May we kindle fires of truth,

May we share the bread of healing,

May God's banquet fill each hand.

      Amen.

20

Space to Rest

Gathering

One: Our spirits are going thirsty;

Our souls are near exhaustion.

All: **We have cancelled the seventh day.**

One: Our agendas are ever-expanding;

Our calendars fill with demands.

All: **We have cancelled the seventh day.**

One: Our breath has no time for the catching;

Our mind has no time for repose.

All: **We have cancelled the seventh day.**

One: Our doing has gained all importance;

Our being has been put on hold.

All: **We have cancelled the seventh day.**

One: Our hearts desire nurture and balance;

Our God shapes a way to respond:

All: **Let there be a seventh day.**

Song: "Come and Find the Quiet Centre"

Readings

GENESIS 2:1-3
Thus the heavens and the earth were finished, and all their multitude. And on the seventh day God finished the work that had been done, and God rested on the seventh day from all the work that had been done. So God blessed the seventh day and hallowed it; because on it God rested from all the work that God had done in creation.

MATTHEW 11:28
Jesus said, "Come unto me, all you that are weary and carrying heavy burdens, and I will give you rest."

DEUTERONOMY 5:12-15
Observe the sabbath day and keep it holy, as God commanded you. Six days you shall labour and do all your work. But the seventh day is a sabbath to God; you shall not do any work — you, or your son or your daughter, or your male or female slave, or your ox or your donkey, or any of your livestock, or the resident alien in your towns.... Remember that you were a slave in the land of Egypt, and God brought you out from there with a mighty hand and an outstretched arm; therefore God commanded you to keep the sabbath day.

I KINGS 19:4-7
Elijah went a day's journey into the wilderness, and came and sat under a solitary broom tree. He asked that he might die: "It is enough; now, O God, take away my life, for I am no better than my ancestors." Then he lay down under the broom tree and fell asleep.

Suddenly an angel touched him and said to him, "Get up and eat." He looked, and there at his head was a cake baked on hot stones, and a jar of water. He ate and drank, and lay down again. The angel of God came a second time, touched him, and said, "Get up and eat, otherwise the journey will be too much for you."

JEREMIAH 31:25
I will satisfy the weary, and all who are faint I will replenish.

MARK 6:31-32
Jesus said to them, "Come away to a deserted place all by your-selves and rest a while." For many were coming and going, and they had no leisure even to eat.

PSALM 18:19
God brought me into a spacious place; God delivered me because God delighted in me.

Response

Time for Quiet Reflection
Participants are invited to reflect silently on how they keep sabbath time in their lives, and how they might want to do this in the future.

Prayer

Spirit of Life:

May we yield to your love,

Resting in your spaciousness,

Mending from our frenzy,

Turning to still waters.

May we trust your quiet rhythm

To calm us back to centre,

To soften brittle places,

To bring new joy in living.

May we receive this sabbath gifting,

May we honour time as friend,

May we listen for your heartbeat,

And bring peace into our own.

Amen.

Song: "Shalom, Chaverim"

Scripture Index

Song Index

Song	Page	Source
Out of the Depths, O God	72	VU
Rise Up, O Saints of God	27, 43	SGP
Shalom, Chaverim	108	SGP
Song of Community	15, 86	SCS
Spirit of Life	48	SCS/VU
Spirit, Spirit of Gentleness	33	SGP/VU
Teach me, God, to Wonder	92	SGP/VU
The Servant Song	88	SGP
The Spirit of the Lord	17	SGP/VU
Thuma Mina	20	VU
("Send me, Lord")		
'Tis the Gift to be Simple	50	
To Abraham and Sarah	11	SGP/VU
To Show by Touch and Word	37	SGP/VU
Trouble and Beauty	5	SCS
Walls that Divide	54	SGP
We are Marching in the Light of God	6	VU

Suggested songs are taken from the following sources:

VU   *Voices United: The Hymn and Worship Book of the United Church of Canada,* John Ambrose, ed. (Etobicoke, Ontario: The United Church Publishing House, 1996).

SGP   *Songs for a Gospel People: A Supplement to The Hymn Book (1971),* R. Gerald Hobbs, ed. (Winfield, B.C.: Wood Lake Books, 1987).

SCS   *Songs for Congregational Singing,* Carolyn McDade, © 1991, c/o 76 Everett Skinner Road, Plainville MA 02762, USA.

Also of interest from The United Church Publishing House

There is a Season: Meditations for Private and Group Worship
Betty Radford Turcott
The themes of justice, peace, and hope are explored in these inspirational devotions, which follow the church year. Each service is complete on two facing pages and includes a call to worship, opening prayer, scripture, suggested popular hymns, a brief meditation, and closing prayer. Suitable for both personal devotion and group worship.

Program Ready: 23 Quick and Complete Programs for the Church Year
Dorothy MacNeill
A collection of programs for every season throughout the church year with ready material for worship, reflection, and discussion. Each program is presented as a complete service and includes a call to worship, scripture, prayers, hymn suggestions, and a short reflection, as well as ideas to spark group activities and discussion.

Telling Her Story: Theology Out of Women's Struggles
Lois Miriam Wilson
"I want to find a way to reconcile my profound love and debt to the biblical record with my emerging awareness of women's struggles towards wholeness. I want to communicate these learnings to children before they get any older," states Wilson. Her popular book is an ideal resource for those who wish to bring new ears and eyes to biblical stories.

Images of Ourselves: The Faith and Work of Canadian Women
photos by Pamela Harris
A book to celebrate The Ecumenical Decade of Churches in Solidarity with Women in Church and Society, *Images of Ourselves* is an acknowledgment and appreciation of the lives and work of women. Included are a gathering of prayers, poems, songs, meditations, and photographs that provides a powerful tool for devotion and renewal.

Crucified Woman
Doris Jean Dyke
In this short and moving book, theologian Doris Jean Dyke tells the powerful story of the impact a statue of a crucified woman had on members of the church and university communities in downtown Toronto. For many, initial feelings of outrage evolved into new feelings and thoughts about traditional Christian doctrine.